THE BIG FAT
Fred
COLLECTION

Since Rupert Fawcett invented Fred eleven years
ago Fred has become something of a star with
books and merchandise in several countries.

Fred's past life is documented in Rupert's twelve
previous books: *Fred*, *More Fred*, *The Extraordinary
World of Fred*, *The Continued Adventures of Fred*,
Carry on Fred, *At Home with Fred*, *Pure Fred*,
The One and Only Fred, *The Little Book of Fred*,
The Best of Fred, *The Second Little Book of Fred*
and *The Best Bits of Fred*.

The Big Fat Fred Collection contains over 400
favourite Fred illustrations depicting Fred's zany life
with the good–natured Penelope and ever–present
black cat, Anthony.

D0996044

Also by Rupert Fawcett published by Headline

CARRY ON FRED

AT HOME WITH FRED

PURE FRED

THE ONE AND ONLY FRED

THE LITTLE BOOK OF FRED

THE BEST OF FRED

THE BEST BITS OF FRED

THE SECOND LITTLE BOOK OF FRED

THE BIG FAT Fred COLLECTION

Rupert Fawcett

HEADLINE

Copyright © 1990, 1991, 1992, 1993, 1994, 1995,
1996, 1997, 1998, 1999, 2000 Rupert Fawcett

The right of Rupert Fawcett to be identified as the Author
of the Work has been asserted by him in accordance with
the Copyright, Designs and Patents Act 1988.

First published in 2000
by HEADLINE BOOK PUBLISHING

10 9 8 7 6 5 4 3 2

All rights reserved. No part of this publication may be
reproduced, stored in a retrieval system, or transmitted, in
any form or by any means without the prior written permission of the publisher, nor be otherwise circulated in
any form of binding or cover other than that in which it is
published and without a similar condition being imposed
on the subsequent purchaser.

ISBN 0 7472 7009 7

Printed and bound by
The Bath Press, Bath

HEADLINE BOOK PUBLISHING
A division of Hodder Headline
338 Euston Road
London NW1 3BH

www.madaboutbooks.co.uk
www.hodderheadline.com

FRED WAS DETERMINED TO PUT THE
YEARS OF UNEMPLOYMENT
BEHIND HIM

THE DOCTOR HAD ADVISED PENELOPE
TO JUST GO ALONG WITH
FRED'S JUMBO JET FANTASY

FRED'S GOLF TECHNIQUE OWED A LOT
TO HIS GREAT SPORTING HERO,
ALEX 'HURRICANE' HIGGINS

UNFORTUNATELY FOR FRED HIS ESCAPE
TUNNEL CAME UP SIX FEET SHORT
OF THE GARDEN FENCE

FRED FELT IT WAS TIME
FOR A CHANGE

FRED ALWAYS HATED IT WHEN PENELOPE
POPPED OUT FOR A CUP OF TEA
WITH THE NEIGHBOURS

IMELDA MARCOS HAD
NOTHING ON FRED

SEEING HIS BOOK IN THE SHOPS FOR THE
FIRST TIME GAVE FRED A TREMENDOUS
FEELING OF ACCOMPLISHMENT

YEARS OF EXPERIENCE HAD TAUGHT
FRED TO STAND WELL BACK WHILE
PENELOPE PREPARED HER BREAKFAST

AS PART OF HER NEW FITNESS PROGRAMME
PENELOPE WATCHED HER JANE FONDA
AEROBICS VIDEO EVERY DAY WITHOUT FAIL

SUCH WAS THE POWER OF FRED'S IMAGINATION
THAT SO FAR AS HE WAS CONCERNED HE
WAS THOMAS THE TANK ENGINE

IT GAVE FRED IMMENSE SATISFACTION
TO RECALL PEOPLE'S SCORNFUL
LAUGHTER WHEN HE FIRST
PLANTED THE LIGHT BULB

FRED WAS READY FOR
THE CAROL SINGERS

FRED COULD ALWAYS DEPEND ON
HIS IN-GROWING TOE NAIL TO
BREAK THE ICE AT PARTIES

FRED'S PRESENT CAME FROM HIS
FAVOURITE GENTLEMAN'S BOUTIQUE

FRED GAVE PIP DIRECTIONS
TO THE BATHROOM

PENELOPE SOMETIMES WISHED FRED
WOULD GET SOME NORMAL FRIENDS

FRED TOOK GREAT CARE TO ESTABLISH
THE PRECISE LOCATION OF HIS
MOTHER-IN-LAW'S HOUSE

IT WAS ANOTHER OF FRED'S
MOUNTAINEERING DREAMS

PENELOPE WAS SURPRISED THAT :-
A. GOD HAD A WIFE, AND
B. SHE WAS SO VAIN

IT WAS A COMFORT TO PENELOPE AND
FRED TO KNOW THAT IF EVER THEY FELL
UPON HARD TIMES THEY WOULD FETCH
A GOOD PRICE FOR GOD'S SLIPPERS

PENELOPE WAS DISMAYED TO SEE
FRED FIGHTING WITH THE
NEXT-DOOR NEIGHBOUR AGAIN

SUCH WAS THE POWER OF FRED'S
SUPERSTITIOUS BELIEFS THAT HE
REFUSED TO GO ANYWHERE WITHOUT
HIS 'LUCKY' WELSH PINE DRESSER

FRED ALWAYS INSISTED ON
HELPING WITH THE GROCERIES

SADLY FOR JIM, THE WEARING OF A
TOUPÉE RESULTED IN HIS IMMEDIATE
EXPULSION FROM BLOBB: THE
BRITISH LEAGUE OF BALD BLOKES

FRED FINALLY DECIDED TO
REPORT THE STALKER

THE TROUBLE WITH HAVING MR AND MRS
JIGSAW AROUND WAS THAT ONE OF
THEM WOULD ALWAYS LOSE A PIECE

'WHY DIDN'T YOU CALL ME SOONER?'
DEMANDED THE CHIN EXPERT

THE DENTAL FLOSS WAS
WELL AND TRULY STUCK

'I BLAME ELTON JOHN,'
WHISPERED PENELOPE

WHEN IT CAME TO DOING THE LAUNDRY
FRED AND PENELOPE MADE
AN EFFICIENT TEAM

'SHE'S HAVING ONE OF HER FAT AND
UGLY DAYS', REPORTED FRED

IT WAS FRED AND PENELOPE'S
FIRST EXPERIENCE OF PET-SWAPPING

FRED HAD FALLEN OUT WITH
THE NEIGHBOURS AGAIN

FRED AND PENELOPE LIKED TO END
THE DAY WITH A NICE GLASS
OF WARM MILK

WITH REGULAR VISITS TO THE PET
CEMETERY FRED WAS GRADUALLY
COMING TO TERMS WITH THE
LOSS OF HIS ANT

CHRISTMAS WAS CELEBRATED WITH ONE OF
FRED'S FAMOUS INDOOR BARBECUES

FRED WAS STILL TRYING TO COME TO
TERMS WITH THE LOSS OF TEDDY

FRED CERTAINLY KNEW HOW TO
TURN PENELOPE ON

FRED SEEMED UNABLE TO CONTAIN HIS
REACTION TO PIP'S NEW 'CARDIE'

FRED WAS INVITED TO SPEAK AT
THE ANNUAL DINNER-DANCE OF
THE ROYAL GUILD OF NOSEPICKERS

FRED BELIEVED THERE WERE THREE
IMPORTANT WORDS IN COOKERY;
PRESENTATION, PRESENTATION
AND PRESENTATION

FRED LIKED TO SPEND HIS WEEKENDS
RELAXING ON THE GOLF COURSE

FRED HAD ALWAYS BEEN SUSPICIOUS
ABOUT PENELOPE'S SO-CALLED
'AEROBICS CLASSES'

FRED WENT TO GREAT LENGTHS TO TRACE
HIS OLD SCHOOL MASTER 'SIX-OF-THE-BEST'
SIMPSON AND INVITE HIM ROUND TO LUNCH

FRED SPENT THE EVENING ADMIRING
HIS CORNFLAKE COLLECTION.

THERE WAS ALWAYS A SMALL PRAYER
BEFORE THE OPENING OF THE
BANK STATEMENT

FRED'S LATEST INVENTION TOOK THE
SWEAT OUT OF BACK-SCRATCHING

PENELOPE'S BREAKFAST ARRIVED AT
THE SAME TIME EVERY MORNING

FRED HAD HEARD THAT PIP
WAS FOND OF FAST FOOD

FRED AND PENELOPE WERE NEVER
AT THEIR BEST FIRST THING
IN THE MORNING

FRED HAD NEVER BEEN WHAT YOU
COULD CALL A 'KEEN' GARDENER

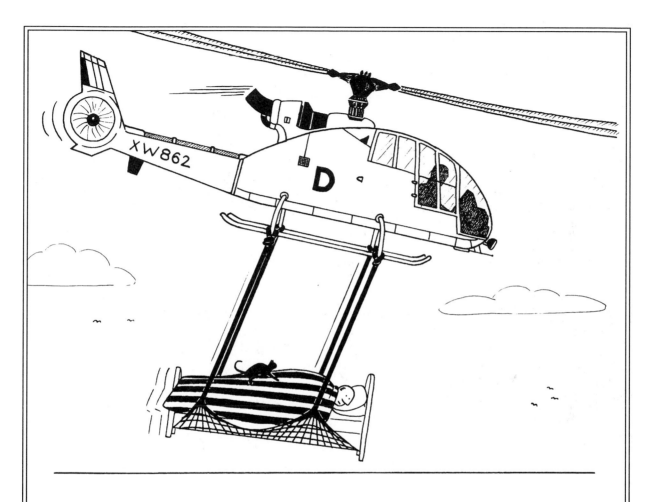

READING 'HOW TO GO TO WORK WITHOUT GETTING OUT OF BED' HAD BEEN A LIFE-CHANGING EXPERIENCE FOR FRED

PENELOPE ASSURED FRED THAT
HE WOULD GROW TO LOVE
THE NEW DECOR

IT WAS TO BE PENELOPE'S
FIRST AND LAST ATTEMPT
AT ROCK CAKES

FRED AND PENELOPE ALWAYS
PROVIDED THEIR GUESTS WITH
AFTER-DINNER ENTERTAINMENT

FRED AND PENELOPE LOVED TO GET
OUT INTO THE COUNTRY AND
STRETCH THEIR LEGS

FRED FOUND THE NEW WINDOW CLEANER
A LITTLE OVER-FAMILIAR

FRED HAD VARIOUS WAYS OF
GETTING RID OF UNWANTED GUESTS

FRED FINALLY REACHED A DECISION
CONCERNING THE CUCKOO CLOCK

FRED SPENT MONTHS RESEARCHING HIS
FORTHCOMING BOOK, 'HOW TO EAT A
SPAGHETTI BOLOGNESE WITHOUT
USING YOUR HANDS'

'NO PEACE FOR THE WICKED',
SIGHED FRED

HAVING BEEN UNABLE TO OBTAIN A LION,
FRED SETTLED FOR THE SLIGHTLY LESS
DANGEROUS PURSUIT OF SLUG-TAMING

WHAT PENELOPE LIKED MOST ABOUT
LIFE WITH FRED WAS THAT THERE WAS
NEVER A DULL MOMENT

WHEN IT CAME TO GARDENING
FRED AND PENELOPE MADE
A GREAT TEAM

FRED AND PENELOPE'S SKATING
PARTIES HAD BECOME A
POPULAR CHRISTMAS EVENT

24 HOUR NON-STOP
EATATHON

CONSTANCE AND PENELOPE LIKED
TO DO THEIR BIT FOR CHARITY

FRED REALISED HE HAD MADE A
BIG MISTAKE BY CALLING
PENELOPE 'CUDDLY'

IT LOOKED LIKE IT WAS GOING
TO BE 'ONE OF THOSE DAYS'

WE CALL IT 'ACUTE SOAP ADDICTION
SYNDROME' WHISPERED THE DOCTOR

FRED OFTEN DREAMED OF DESIGNING
A GOLF COURSE OF HIS OWN

FRED AND PENELOPE HAD ALWAYS
SENSED THAT BOB WOULD HAVE
LIKED TO HAVE BEEN MORE
THAN JUST A MILKMAN

AS THEY DEPARTED, FRED'S
GUESTS WERE EACH ISSUED WITH
A COMMEMORATIVE 'T' SHIRT

PENELOPE KINDLY AGREED TO ASSIST
FRED WITH RESEARCH FOR HIS
FORTHCOMING BOOK, 'A DAY IN THE
LIFE OF A ROLLING PIN'

PENELOPE HAD A TENDENCY TO
MONOPOLISE THE BISCUIT BARREL

FRED AND PENELOPE'S GUESTS
COULD ALWAYS BE SURE OF
A WARM WELCOME

PENELOPE WAS RELIEVED THAT FRED
HAD AT LAST AGREED TO ATTEND
'ROAD-RAGE' COUNSELLING

HAVING OVERCOME THEIR INITIAL
SHYNESS FRED AND THE CREATURE
FROM THE DEEP FOUND THEY ACTUALLY
HAD QUITE A LOT IN COMMON

WHERE PIP'S SOCKS WERE CONCERNED
THE KEY WORD WAS 'CAUTION'

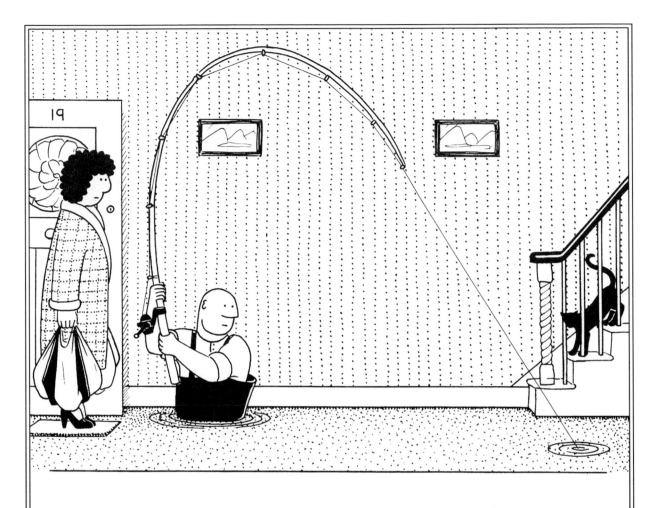

LIFE WITH FRED WAS FULL OF
THE UNEXPECTED

ONCE OR TWICE A YEAR FRED GOT
TOGETHER WITH HIS OLD SCHOOL
PALS ,'BEAKY' BALDWIN ,'SMARMY'
SMITH AND 'EMBARRASSING' ED

IT SEEMED A CRUEL IRONY THAT
TINY WAS THE ONLY PERSON UNABLE
TO ATTEND HIS OWN BIRTHDAY PARTY

PIP HAD ALWAYS BEEN A BIG
FAN OF PENELOPE'S SOUPS

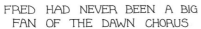

FRED HAD NEVER BEEN A BIG
FAN OF THE DAWN CHORUS

WHILE PENELOPE PREPARED THE DINNER
FRED LOOKED AFTER THE GUESTS

ON THE FIRST DAY OF HIS NEW JOB
FRED EXPERIENCED A FEW
TEETHING PROBLEMS

BOB AND PENELOPE ALWAYS GOT
VERY TORVILL AND DEAN ABOUT
THE MILK BILL

FRED WAS DISMAYED TO DISCOVER
HIS NEWSAGENT HAD COMPLETELY
SOLD OUT OF 'WHAT TROUSERS'?

FRED HAD NEVER SHARED PENELOPE'S
ENTHUSIASM FOR CHRISTMAS SHOPPING

FRED REALISED HE HAD BEEN A FOOL
TO UNDERESTIMATE THE POWER
OF PENELOPE'S KICK

FRED WAS QUITE HAPPY TO HAVE PENELOPE'S
MOTHER TO STAY FOR CHRISTMAS SO LONG
AS SHE WAS ON HER MEDICATION

FRED AND PIP ALWAYS GREETED
EACH OTHER WITH THE SECRET
HANDSHAKE OF B.L.O.B.B. ; THE
BRITISH LEAGUE OF BALD BLOKES

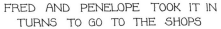

FRED AND PENELOPE TOOK IT IN
TURNS TO GO TO THE SHOPS

'THEY CAN KEEP THEIR SEAN CONNERYS
AND HARRISON FORDS', SIGHED PENELOPE

FRED THOUGHT A LITTLE MUSIC
MIGHT SOOTHE PENELOPE'S MIGRAINE

'AS SOON AS HE GETS BEHIND
THE WHEEL OF A CAR HE TURNS
INTO A COMPLETE ANIMAL',
SIGHED PENELOPE

PENELOPE SO ENJOYED BACK-SEAT
DRIVING THAT SHE DECIDED TO HAVE
THE CAR SPECIALLY MODIFIED

FRED WAS ONLY PREPARED TO
TAKE HIS MOTHER-IN-LAW ON
HOLIDAY ON CERTAIN CONDITIONS

FRED AND PENELOPE'S MORNING
ABLUTIONS WERE CHOREOGRAPHED
TO PERFECTION

BEFORE BEING ALLOWED INTO BED
PENELOPE WAS ALWAYS REQUIRED TO
SHOW SOME FORM OF IDENTIFICATION

THE BEST GLASSES ONLY CAME OUT
ON VERY SPECIAL OCCASIONS

PENELOPE COULDN'T HELP FEELING THAT
FRED'S ATTEMPT AT LANDSCAPE
GARDENING LACKED IMAGINATION

AFTER MONTHS OF WAITING, FRED
AND PENELOPE FINALLY RECEIVED
PLANNING PERMISSION FOR THEIR
NASAL EXTENSIONS

FRED FINALLY FINISHED THE
GRANNY ANNEXE

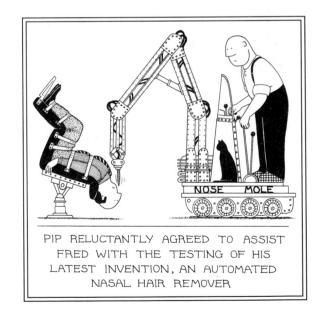

PIP RELUCTANTLY AGREED TO ASSIST
FRED WITH THE TESTING OF HIS
LATEST INVENTION, AN AUTOMATED
NASAL HAIR REMOVER

'HE'S FAILED TO MAKE THE HONOURS
LIST AGAIN', SIGHED PENELOPE

MR AND MRS NESBIT NEVER TIRED OF
HEARING ABOUT FRED AND PENELOPE'S
1973 HOLIDAY IN SPAIN

ONCE A MONTH FRED WOULD GET
TOGETHER WITH HIS FISHING PALS

FRED HAD PROMISED TO GET
MR AND MRS NESBIT HOME IN TIME
FOR THE ARCHERS

FRED COULD ALWAYS TELL WHEN
THE GOLDFISH WERE ARGUING

ON THE WEEKENDS FRED AND
PIP LIKED TO UNWIND WITH A
FEW GAMES OF PING

IT WAS TIME FOR WALKIES

ABOUT TEN DAYS AFTER FRED'S VISIT
TO THE DOCTOR PENELOPE COULD
SENSE HIS ANTI-DEPRESSANTS
BEGINNING TO KICK IN

IF FRED AND PENELOPE'S FIRST B+B
CUSTOMER HAD ONE COMPLAINT, IT
WOULD SIMPLY BE THAT THEY WERE
TRYING A LITTLE TOO HARD

IF THE TRUTH BE KNOWN, FRED
WAS SICK TO DEATH OF PENELOPE'S
GARDEN FURNITURE BURGERS

FRED AND PENELOPE COULDN'T HELP
NOTICING THAT THE NEIGHBOURHOOD
WAS BECOMING MORE VIOLENT

FRED AND PENELOPE WONDERED WHAT
HAD BECOME OF THEIR GUESTS SINCE THEY
FINISHED THEIR CHRISTMAS DINNER

PENELOPE WAS DETERMINED NOT TO BE
PUT OFF BY HER FIRST EXPERIENCE
OF BAKING

PENELOPE WAS A GREAT BELIEVER
IN THE POWER OF PRAYER

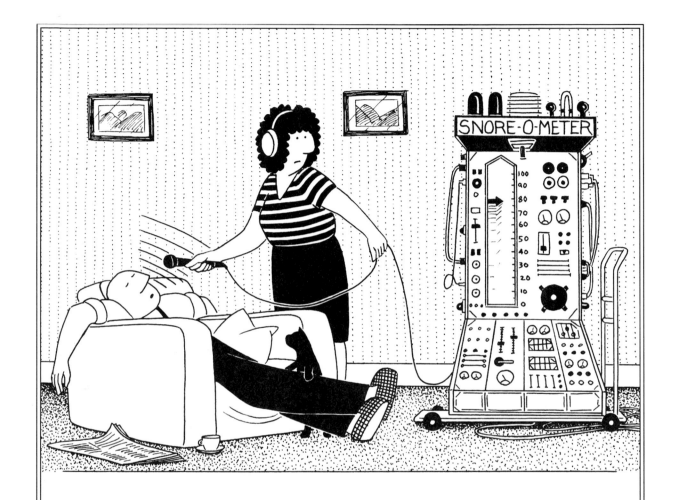

PENELOPE WAS BUSY ACCUMULATING
EVIDENCE FOR HER NOISE POLLUTION
COMPENSATION CLAIM

FRED AND PENELOPE LOVED TO
EXPERIMENT WITH NEW
PAINT TECHNIQUES

PENELOPE COULDN'T HELP THINKING
THE CHIPPENDALES AUDITION
WOULD END IN TEARS

FRED WAS THRILLED THAT THE
LOCAL AMATEUR DRAMATIC SOCIETY
HAD FINALLY GIVEN HIM A PART

PENELOPE COULDN'T HELP FEELING
THAT FRED WASN'T ENTERING
INTO THE TRUE SPIRIT OF
THE ADVENTURE HOLIDAY

AFTER MONTHS OF PREPARATION
SHOOTING FINALLY GOT UNDERWAY ON
'FRED — THE INGROWING TOE NAIL'

FRED WAS TIRED OF HEARING PIP
WHINGEING ABOUT THE BUNGEE JUMP

SUNDAY WAS SPENT TESTING
FRED'S LATEST INVENTION, THE
WALK 'N' PAINT CEILING ROLLER

SATURDAY NIGHT
WAS LOTTERY NIGHT

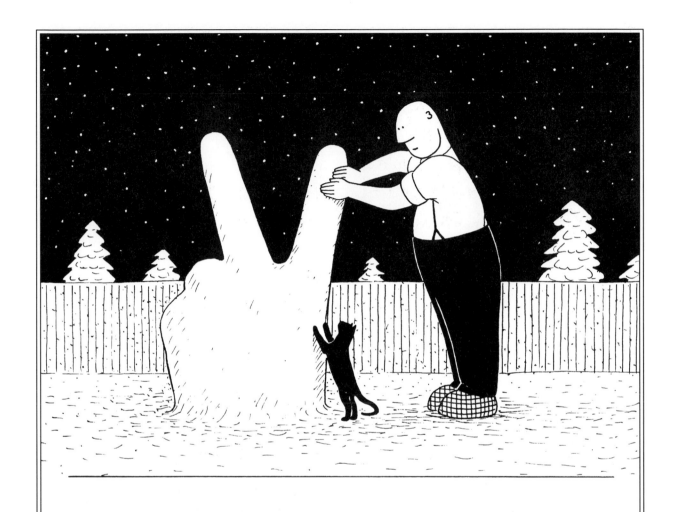

FRED SPENT THE AFTERNOON WORKING ON
HIS CHRISTMAS MESSAGE TO THE NATION

EVERYBODY WAS ASKED TO WAIT
PATIENTLY FOR THEIR TURN WITH
THE SCATTER CUSHIONS

PENELOPE SOMETIMES WISHED FRED PUT
AS MUCH ENERGY INTO THEIR MARRIAGE
AS HE DID INTO HIS HOBBIES

FRED WAS DISAPPOINTED TO SEE A
TRUSTED FRIEND BREAKING THE RULES

PENELOPE THOUGHT SHE COULD DETECT
THE TELL-TALE SIGNS OF A
MID-LIFE CRISIS

FRED'S LATEST INVENTION WAS DESIGNED
TO DO THE WORK OF TEN MEN

FRED AND PENELOPE SPENT THE
AFTERNOON ENGROSSED IN THEIR
CHRISTMAS PRESENTS

FRED FOUND THAT BEING
HAUNTED WASN'T ALL BAD

WHILE PENELOPE PREPARED THE DINNER
FRED LOOKED AFTER THE DRINKS

PENELOPE COULDN'T HELP FEELING
THAT FRED WAS OVER-REACTING
TO THE GREENFLY

'I BLAME ALL THOSE S.A.S. BOOKS
HE'S BEEN READING', SIGHED PENELOPE

IT WAS SO LONG SINCE FRED HAD
SEEN IT THAT PENELOPE VERY KINDLY
AGREED TO DESCRIBE IT TO HIM

THE REACTION TO FRED'S HOMEMADE
LEMONADE WAS UNIFORM

FRED SPENT THE AFTERNOON RESEARCHING HIS
FORTHCOMING BOOK, 'ONE THOUSAND WAYS
TO EAT A FLAPJACK'

FRED HAD AN UNINTERRUPTED
VIEW OF PIP'S CAR BEING
WHEEL-CLAMPED

FRED FINALLY GOT LUCKY DOWN
AT THE JOB CENTRE

FRED AND PENELOPE'S NEW BATHROOM
MIRROR WAS GOING TO TAKE
SOME GETTING USED TO

PENELOPE'S 'IT'S TEDDY OR ME' ULTIMATUM
APPEARED TO HAVE BACKFIRED

FRED WAS EXPERIENCING SOME
DIFFICULTY WITH HIS NEW
'ECONOMY SIZE' PEN

AT LAST THE MAN ARRIVED
ABOUT THE DAMP

FRED'S STRAP-ON CHAIRS ALLOWED HIS
GUESTS TO MOVE FROM THE LOUNGE
TO THE DINING TABLE WITHOUT HAVING
TO LEAVE THEIR SEATS

FRED HAD AN UNQUENCHABLE
THIRST FOR ADVENTURE

FRED LOVED ENTERTAINING

PENELOPE COULDN'T WAIT TO SEE
WHAT FRED HAD PREPARED FOR
HER SURPRISE BIRTHDAY DINNER

FRED AND PENELOPE
MADE A GREAT TEAM

IT WAS ANOTHER OF FRED'S
BOUNCY CASTLE DREAMS

IT WAS A CLASSIC CASE
OF LAWN RAGE

FRED HAD A KEEN INTEREST IN
MODERN ENGLISH LITERATURE

PENELOPE ALWAYS PUT A
LOT OF THOUGHT INTO
FRED'S CHRISTMAS PRESENT

FRED SPENT CHRISTMAS EVE
PREPARING FOR THE ARRIVAL
OF HIS IN-LAWS

AFTER TEA PENELOPE SAT DOWN
WITH HER KNITTING WHILE FRED
GOT ON WITH A SPOT OF D.I.Y.

MONDAY STARTED BADLY

DURING TESTING OF HIS LATEST
INVENTION, THE 'WINTER DOGGY
SUIT' FRED REALISED IT HAD
ONE GLARING DESIGN FAULT

FRED MODIFIED HIS LAWNMOWER
SO THAT EVERY TIME HE USED
IT HE AUTOMATICALLY GOT
A PAT ON THE BACK

AFTER A COUPLE OF GLASSES OF
WINE FRED COULD SENSE PENELOPE
BEGINNING TO UNWIND

PENELOPE SOON REALISED THAT THE
ADVENTURE HOLIDAY WAS
WASTED ON FRED

BY THE FOURTH DAY OF THEIR
HOLIDAY FRED AND PENELOPE
COULD FEEL THEMSELVES
BEGINNING TO UNWIND

PENELOPE OFTEN REQUIRED A
LITTLE EXTRA HELP WITH GETTING
UP IN THE MORNING

IT ALWAYS MADE PENELOPE SAD
TO SEE FRED MIGRATE

PENELOPE HAD ALWAYS SUSPECTED
THAT FRED HAD ANOTHER LIFE

FRED HAD BEEN LOOKING FORWARD TO
HIS BIRTHDAY PARTY FOR MONTHS

HIGH ON EVERY TOURIST'S ITINERARY
WAS A TRIP TO FRED'S HOUSE TO SEE
'THE CHANGING OF THE SHEETS'

PENELOPE INSISTED ON
EXTREMELY SAFE SEX

FRED AND PENELOPE'S MARRIAGE WAS
GOING THROUGH ONE OF ITS
DIFFICULT PHASES

BY THE SECOND BOTTLE OF WINE
FRED AND PENELOPE'S MILLENNIUM
CELEBRATION WAS STARTING
TO GO WITH A SWING

FRED ALWAYS MADE A BIT OF A DRAMA
OUT OF CARVING THE SUNDAY JOINT

FRED LIKED TO THINK OF HIMSELF
AS AN ENTREPRENEUR

WHEN FRED ORGANISED A REUNION OF
HIS OLD PRIMARY SCHOOL PALS HE
WAS DELIGHTED TO DISCOVER
THAT THEY HADN'T CHANGED A BIT

FROM THE MOMENT HE WAS
BORN FRED SEEMED SOMEHOW
DIFFERENT FROM OTHER BABIES

TO AVOID THE HASSLE OF WALKING
AROUND THE END OF THE BED
TO REACH THE BATHROOM FRED
CONSTRUCTED A SMALL BRIDGE

WHILE FRED ENJOYED HIS WINE
TASTING PENELOPE BECAME
INCREASINGLY INTERESTED
IN 'J' CLOTH SNIFFING

PENELOPE COULD NEVER RESIST A
MAN IN A NEW PAIR OF SLIPPERS

FRED COULDN'T HELP FEELING
THAT HIS LIFE WAS
DISAPPOINTINGLY DULL

FOR HER BIRTHDAY PENELOPE
HAD ASKED FRED FOR A
PAIR OF MULES

FRED STILL YEARNED FOR HIS
OLD DAYS AT THE ZOO

FRED SAT DOWN TO ENJOY
A SPOT OF LUNCH.

PENELOPE SENT FRED UPSTAIRS
FOR THE BIG TEAPOT.

FRED DIDN'T LIKE BIG
DISPLAYS OF EMOTION

FRED COULD FEEL A
NOVEL COMING ON.

PIP WAS BECOMING SUSPICIOUS
ABOUT FRED'S SO-CALLED
LUCKY STREAK

PENELOPE HAD FOUND
HER VOCATION

FRED SPENT THE AFTERNOON
JOB-HUNTING

PIP HAD DROPPED CRUMBS ON THE
CARPET ONCE TOO OFTEN

WHEN IT CAME TO THEIR GARDEN
FRED AND PENELOPE
WERE PERFECTIONISTS

CABINET WAR ROOM

PENELOPE AND THE GIRLS NEVER
GAVE UP IN THEIR BATTLE
AGAINST CELLULITE

FRED AND PENELOPE FELT THEY
HAD TO CLIMB THE STAIRCASE
SIMPLY BECAUSE IT WAS THERE

IT WAS ANOTHER OF FRED'S
PAISLEY ATTACKS

ANTHONY'S FRIENDS WERE
A CLASSY CROWD

EVERY SUMMER FRED AND PENELOPE
LIKED TO GET AWAY FROM IT ALL

RELATIONS WITH THE NEIGHBOURS
SEEMED TO BE DETERIORATING

BY TRAVELLING 'SUPER ECONOMY' FRED
AND PENELOPE WERE ABLE TO AFFORD
A LITTLE HOLIDAY ABROAD

WHEN FRED HAD FINISHED HIS
IMPRESSIONS THE AUDIENCE
GAVE HIM A BIG HAND

JEREMY'S PREDICAMENT CLEARLY
ILLUSTRATED THE DANGER OF
STANDING CLOSE TO TREES FOR
LONG PERIODS OF TIME

AFTER MONTHS OF UNEMPLOYMENT
FRED AND PENELOPE WERE FORCED
TO SELL THEIR HOUSE AND 'DOWNSIZE'

ALTHOUGH EVERYBODY LOVED FRED
THEY EACH HAD THEIR OWN
FAVOURITE BIT

FRED HAD FALLEN OUT WITH
THE NEIGHBOURS AGAIN

FRED'S EVENING OF DANCE AND
MIME CLIMAXED WITH HIS MUCH
ACCLAIMED 'ANGLEPOISE LAMP'

THINGS HADN'T BEEN THE SAME
SINCE PENELOPE DID HER
ASSERTIVENESS TRAINING COURSE

FRED WAS FINDING
MARRIAGE TO PENELOPE
INCREASINGLY CLAUSTROPHOBIC

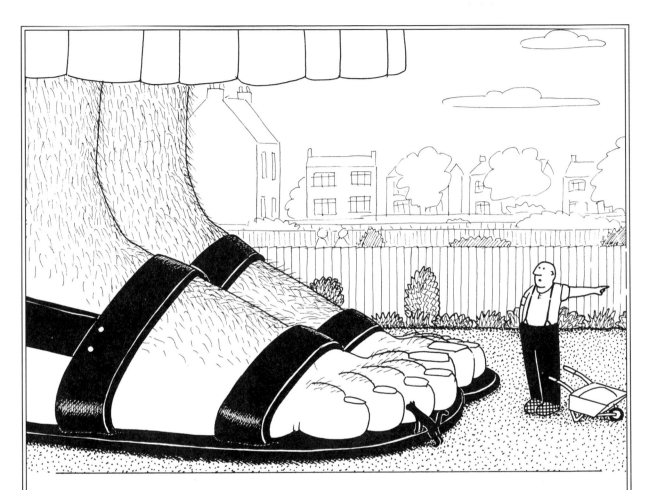

CONSIDERING HE WAS SUPPOSED TO
BE ALL-SEEING AND ALL-KNOWING
FRED WAS SURPRISED THAT GOD
NEEDED DIRECTIONS TO THE CHIP SHOP

FRED WISHED BOB WOULD JUST LEAVE
IT ON THE STEP LIKE OTHER MILKMEN

PENELOPE HATED TO BE DISTURBED
DURING HER FAVOURITE SOAP

FRED SOMEHOW MANAGED TO GET
HIMSELF CAUGHT UP IN THE
WRONG DEMO

'HE'S ALWAYS LIKE THIS FOR A FEW HOURS
AFTER HIS OBEDIENCE CLASS, THEN IT'S
BACK TO HIS OLD WAYS', SIGHED MR NESBIT

IF HIS FIRST DAY WAS ANYTHING TO
GO BY FRED'S CAREER AS A TREE
SURGEON WOULD BE SHORTLIVED

NOBODY EVER SAID A WORD ABOUT
MRS NESBIT'S LITTLE PROBLEM

FRED THANKED BOB FOR THE
EXTRA PINT OF GOLD-TOP

PIP HAD KNOWN THERE WOULD BE
A PRICE TO PAY FOR TAKING
FRED'S LAST HUMBUG

FRED LOVED TO CURL UP
WITH A GOOD BOOK

FRED OFTEN WISHED PENELOPE
HADN'T INTRODUCED PIP TO HER
ASSERTIVENESS TRAINING CLASSES

'I CAN'T DO A THING WITH HIM',
SIGHED PENELOPE

FRED FINALLY CONFESSED TO
EATING THE SOFA.

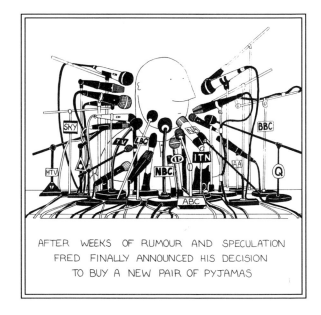

AFTER WEEKS OF RUMOUR AND SPECULATION
FRED FINALLY ANNOUNCED HIS DECISION
TO BUY A NEW PAIR OF PYJAMAS

FRED COULDN'T HELP FEELING THAT
PENELOPE WAS MAKING THE KITCHEN
A LITTLE TOO HYGIENIC

FRED'S VEGETARIAN DIET WAS
TAKING SOME GETTING USED TO

FRED'S BAND, 'THE SILENTS' CONSISTED
OF JIM ON AIR GUITAR, FRED ON AIR
BASS, PIP ON AIR DRUMS AND
MR NESBIT ON AIR TRIANGLE

FOR A SMALL FEE A FEW HAND-
PICKED INDIVIDUALS WERE ALLOWED
INTO THE HOUSE EACH MORNING
TO WATCH FRED EAT HIS PORRIDGE

PENELOPE WAS BECOMING CONCERNED
ABOUT FRED'S DRINKING

ONCE AGAIN THE SECRETARY OF THE
EXCLUSIVE 'POINTY HAT AND NOSE
CLUB' WAS FORCED TO REMIND PIP
OF THEIR STRICT DRESS CODE

FRED WAS GOING FOR GOLD

AFTER LUNCH FRED TREATED HIS
CHRISTMAS GUESTS TO AN INDOOR
FIREWORK DISPLAY

FRED'S FAVOURITE EVENT AT
THE HIGHLAND GAMES WAS
TOSSING THE WIFE

PENELOPE WAS DISAPPOINTED TO
SEE FRED AND HER MOTHER
FIGHTING AGAIN

FRED WAS BECOMING INCREASINGLY
CONCERNED ABOUT PENELOPE'S EYESIGHT

EVEN AS A BOY THE WORLD HAD
SEEMED STRANGE TO FRED

POPPING OVER TO THE NESBITS
FOR TEA AND SCONES WAS NEVER
QUITE AS SIMPLE AS IT SOUNDED

HAVING VISITED LOURDES AND THE SHROUD
OF TURIN, FRED AND PENELOPE THEN
MADE A PILGRIMAGE TO THE LATEST BIG
ATTRACTION ON THE RELIGIOUS MAP

CONSIDERING FRED AND PENELOPE HAD
ONLY ATTENDED ONE YOGA CLASS
THEY WERE DOING WELL

FRED AND PENELOPE SPENT ANOTHER
EVENING IN THE FAST LANE

ALL FRED HAD EVER KNOWN ABOUT
HIS SECOND COUSIN WAS THAT HE
WAS 'SOMETHING BIG IN THE CITY'

FRED ALWAYS HATED HAVING
HIS EYES TESTED

EVERY SUMMER FRED AND PENELOPE
LIKED TO GET AWAY FROM IT ALL

PENELOPE WAS BEGINNING TO WISH
SHE HAD NEVER BOUGHT FRED
THE CAMCORDER

FROM TIME TO TIME FRED WOULD
TAKE THE MORE ADVENTUROUS
ROUTE TO THE NEWSAGENT

PENELOPE'S KEEP-FIT CAMPAIGN
GOT OFF TO A GENTLE START

IT WAS TIME FOR FRED'S INTERVIEW
DOWN AT THE JOB CENTRE

PENELOPE COULDN'T WAIT TO SEE
FRED'S REACTION TO HER SENSUOUS
NEW PERFUME, 'SEDUCTION IN PARIS'

FRED DERIVED IMMENSE PLEASURE
FROM SITTING IN THE BATH FOR
EXTENDED PERIODS AND WATCHING
EVERYTHING GO WRINKLY

FRED ASKED MR AND MRS NESBIT
TO LEAVE VIA THE SECRET TUNNEL.

EVERYONE EAGERLY AWAITED A SLICE OF
PENELOPE'S UPSIDE-DOWN CAKE

WHILE FRED WAS AT HIS DARTS PRACTICE
PENELOPE DECIDED TO TREAT HERSELF
TO AN INDIAN

FRED WAS INTRIGUED BY
PENELOPE'S LATEST HOBBY

'THIS IS THE LAST TIME WE
TRAVEL SUPER-ECONOMY',
SPAT PENELOPE

HAVING GROWN BORED WITH SLUG-TAMING
FRED DECIDED TO TRY HIS HAND
AT WORM-CHARMING

FRED WAS DETERMINED TO PUT THE
YEARS OF UNEMPLOYMENT BEHIND HIM

FRED HAD ALWAYS SUSPECTED THERE
WAS ANOTHER SIDE TO MRS NESBIT

FRED WROTE THE
SHOPPING LIST WITH
HIS NEW WATERPROOF PEN.

'SO THIS IS THE SIXTY-NINE
POSITION', SAID FRED GRIMLY.

FRED AND PIP WERE THE KINDA GUYS
THAT LIKED TO WORK HARD
AND PLAY HARD

FRED 'FLOSSED' HIS GUESTS
BETWEEN EACH COURSE.

FRED GREW ACCUSTOMED TO
PENELOPE'S TANTRUMS

PENELOPE SOMETIMES WISHED FRED
COULD GET HIMSELF A NORMAL
HOBBY LIKE GOLF OR FISHING

MOST BORING MAN IN THE
WORLD COMPETITION

PIP WAS GOING FOR GOLD

THE SPECIALLY TRAINED OFFICER SPENT
SEVERAL HOURS TRYING TO COAX PIP
DOWN FROM THE COFFEE TABLE

AS USUAL IT WAS 'STANDING
ROOM ONLY' FOR THE CHANGING
OF THE LIGHT-BULB

AT LAST FRED FOUND
THE PERFECT JOB

FRED ADORED COMPETITIONS

AS USUAL THERE WAS SOME
DISAGREEMENT OVER WHO SHOULD
HAVE THE LAST JAFFA CAKE

FRED OFTEN WONDERED WHY A GOOD-
LOOKING CHAP LIKE PENELOPE'S COUSIN
FRANK NEVER HAD ANY GIRLFRIENDS

THIS IS WHERE FRED KEEPS HIS
STAGE-GEAR REVEALED PENELOPE

'ONE WINE GUM AND HE'S ANYBODY'S',
GROANED PENELOPE

FRED LIKED NOTHING MORE THAN A
RELAXING AFTERNOON'S FISHING

FRED AND PENELOPE SPENT
MANY HAPPY EVENINGS RE-LIVING
THEIR HONEYMOON IN VENICE

FRED COULDN'T HELP FEELING
THAT PIP WAS OVER-REACTING
TO HIS £10 LOTTERY WIN

PIP WAS FINALLY INITIATED INTO THE
SECRET TOMATO KETCHUP CLUB

FRED ALWAYS LIKED TO GET
AWAY AT CHRISTMAS

THE BABY POLTERGEIST WAS BACK.

FRED SENSED THAT ALL WAS
NOT WELL WITH PIP.

PIP WISHED HE HAD NEVER AGREED TO
HELP FRED WITH THE PRUNING

FRED WAS FORCED TO REMIND HIS LODGER OF THE 'NO ELEPHANTS' CLAUSE IN THEIR TENANCY AGREEMENT

APPARENTLY FRED AND THE BURGLAR HAD BEEN AT SCHOOL TOGETHER

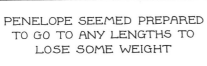

PENELOPE SEEMED PREPARED TO GO TO ANY LENGTHS TO LOSE SOME WEIGHT

PENELOPE HAD OFTEN HEARD IT SAID THAT THE WAY TO A MAN'S HEART WAS THROUGH HIS STOMACH

FRED WAS ALWAYS PLEASED
TO SEE THE NESBITS

PENELOPE WONDERED HOW LONG
IT WOULD TAKE FRED TO NOTICE
HER NEW HAIRSTYLE

FRED HAD NEVER BEEN
A MORNINGS PERSON

FRED AND PENELOPE'S NEWSAGENT
CATERED TO ALL TASTES

FOR MANY YEARS FRED'S SECRET SUNDAY
AFTERNOON NAPS WENT UNDETECTED

PENELOPE FOUND HERSELF WONDERING
WHY SHE HADN'T SIMPLY GONE TO
HER CHIROPODIST APPOINTMENT
BY BUS

AT LAST PENELOPE FOUND THE
PERFECT WAY TO KEEP FIT,
'VIRTUAL AEROBICS'

IT WAS ONE OF PENELOPE'S
'BAD HAIR' DAYS

FRED AND PENELOPE FELT SURE THAT
BEFORE TOO LONG THE BANK MANAGER
WOULD BEGIN TO SEE THINGS
FROM THEIR POINT OF VIEW

MONDAY WAS WASHDAY

FRED HAD BEEN WARNED ABOUT
LEAVING THE LAVATORY SEAT UP

THE EVENING WAS SPENT TESTING
PENELOPE'S NEW LABOUR-SAVING
LIPSTICK APPLICATOR.

'LAST WEEK IT WAS MARLON
BRANDO, THIS WEEK MICHAEL
CAINE,' WHISPERED PENELOPE

PIP LOOKED ALL SET TO WIN THE
DOG-OWNER LOOK-A-LIKE CONTEST

BUNTY ALWAYS SPENT HOURS
DRESSING FOR A PARTY

'THAT'S HIS SEVENTEENTH ROLY-POLY
STRIPPAGRAM THIS WEEK DOCTOR',
FRETTED PENELOPE

FRED LIKED TO KEEP ABREAST
OF CURRENT AFFAIRS

PIP'S APPLICATION TO JOIN THE GENTLEMEN'S
ZIG-ZAG CLUB WAS REJECTED DUE TO
'INSUFFICIENT VISIBLE ZIG-ZAGS'

FRED TOOK ADVANTAGE OF HIS FAMILY'S
CHRISTMAS VISIT TO CARRY OUT SOME
URGENT ROOF REPAIRS

FRED AND PENELOPE OPTED FOR A
QUIET EVENING AT HOME WITH
THE CHAINSAWS

AS USUAL THE MEN SPENT THE
EVENING TALKING BALLS

'FRED'S BEEN TALKING TO
THEM AGAIN', SIGHED PENELOPE

'IF YOU SEE THE MAN WHO POKED HIS TONGUE
OUT AT YOU JUST PLACE YOUR HAND ON HIS
SHOULDER', WHISPERED DETECTIVE DOBSON OF
THE CHEEKY BEHAVIOUR SQUAD

FRED WAS DETERMINED TO PROVE THE
EXISTENCE OF THE MONSTER

PENELOPE WAS NOT AT ALL
HAPPY WITH FRED'S PENCHANT
FOR VIRTUAL BATHS

PEOPLE CAME FROM FAR AND WIDE
FOR A GLIMPSE OF PENELOPE'S
DUST BALLS

PENELOPE CERTAINLY KNEW HOW
TO MAKE FRED FEEL SMALL

FRED'S LIFE WAS ALWAYS
FULL OF DRAMA

AS THEIR NEW LODGER UNPACKED HIS
BELONGINGS FRED AND PENELOPE
BECAME APPREHENSIVE

FRED AND PENELOPE TRIED VARIOUS
WAYS OF MAKING THE WALK TO
THE LIBRARY MORE INTERESTING

PENELOPE FINALLY DECIDED TO
DO SOMETHING ABOUT FRED'S
OVER-SLEEPING PROBLEM

PENELOPE WONDERED WHAT SORT
OF RESTAURANT FRED HAD IN MIND FOR
THEIR ROMANTIC VALENTINE DINNER

FRED'S WAVE MACHINE TOOK THE
EFFORT OUT OF FAREWELLS

PENELOPE HAD BECOME CONCERNED
ABOUT FRED SINCE HE LOST THE
KNOBBLY KNEES CONTEST

FRED FOUND THE NEW COFFEE
TABLE SUSPICIOUSLY QUIET

'I GOT THIS ONE FOR WASHING THE CAR AND MOWING THE LAWN IN THE SAME DAY,' EXPLAINED FRED

WHILE PENELOPE SERVED THE
HORS D'OEUVRES, FRED ENTERTAINED
THEIR GUESTS WITH THE STORY OF
HIS IN-GROWING TOE NAIL

FRED COULDN'T HELP FEELING THAT
THE MILKMAN WAS BECOMING A
LITTLE OVER-FAMILIAR

'LOOKS LIKE TINY HAS FORGOTTEN
HIS GLOVES AGAIN', REMARKED FRED

PENELOPE WONDERED IF BUNTY MIGHT BENEFIT FROM A MORE SUBTLE APPROACH

FRED INVITED HIS GUESTS INTO THE BATHROOM TO PLAY HUNT - THE - SOAP

IT WAS ANOTHER OF PENELOPE'S TINA TURNER DREAMS

IT WAS SAD BUT TRUE : VERA REALLY DID HAVE A FACE LIKE THE BACK OF A BUS

AFTER WEEKS OF NEGLECT FRED AND
PENELOPE'S BACK GARDEN HAD BECOME
A BIT OF A JUNGLE

FRED AND PENELOPE WERE BEGINNING
TO WISH THEY'D NEVER HEARD THE NAME
'CHEEKY BATHROOM MIRRORS INCORPORATED'

PENELOPE'S DIET RESTRICTED HER TO
JUST ONE MINCE PIE OVER CHRISTMAS

FRED'S QUICK REFLEXES SAVED
THE SAUSAGE ROLLS.

FRED WAS FAMOUS FOR HIS
CHRISTMAS BARBECUES

FRED ASKED CONSTANCE
AND PIP NOT TO WALK
ON THE NEW CARPET.

'WE CALL IT 'TINA TURNER SYNDROME,'
SAID THE DOCTOR GRAVELY

FRED AND PENELOPE PROVIDED
THEIR GUESTS WITH AFTER-
DINNER ENTERTAINMENT.

FRED SHOWED MR AND MRS NESBIT
TO THE GUEST ROOM

FRED WAS EXPERIENCING THE FAMOUS 'BOBBLE-HAT EFFECT'

PIP WAS BEGINNING TO WISH HE'D NEVER MENTIONED THE MOTH

PIP HAD EVIDENTLY BECOME INCREASINGLY BORING DURING THE COURSE OF THE YEAR

AT TIMES THE TABLE FOOTBALL COULD GET QUITE DIRTY

AFTER DINNER EVERYONE PLAYED
SPOT-THE-CAT

FRED WAS HOPELESS UNITED'S
MOST LOYAL SUPPORTER

FRED HAD NEVER SHARED
PENELOPE'S ENTHUSIASM
FOR SHOPPING

SADLY, DUE TO LACK OF BUSINESS
ANOTHER FRED ENTERPRISE WAS
ABOUT TO GO 'BELLY UP'

FRED SPENT THE EVENING WORKING OUT HOW MUCH MONEY HE HAD SAVED BY DOING THE PLUMBING HIMSELF

WHILE PENELOPE READ HER GLOSSIES
FRED GOT ON WITH A SPOT
OF GARDENING

FRED WAS BEGINNING TO GET
FED UP WITH PENELOPE'S
VIRTUAL DINNERS

FRED SERVED COFFEE IN THE
TROPHY ROOM

FRED AND PENELOPE WONDERED WHAT
HAD BECOME OF THEIR GUESTS SINCE THEY
FINISHED THEIR CHRISTMAS DINNER

'HE'S BEEN LIKE THIS EVER
SINCE HE LOST TINKY-WINKY',
WHISPERED PENELOPE

PIP WAS BEGINNING TO WISH HE
HAD NEVER AGREED TO HELP
FRED LAUNCH HIS LATEST
BUSINESS VENTURE

'THIS IS THE LAST TIME WE
EMPLOY COWBOY BUILDERS',
RESOLVED FRED

IT TOOK A LOT TO DISTRACT
FRED FROM HIS NEWSPAPER

PENELOPE SEEMED TO TAKE
AGES PUTTING ON HER FACE

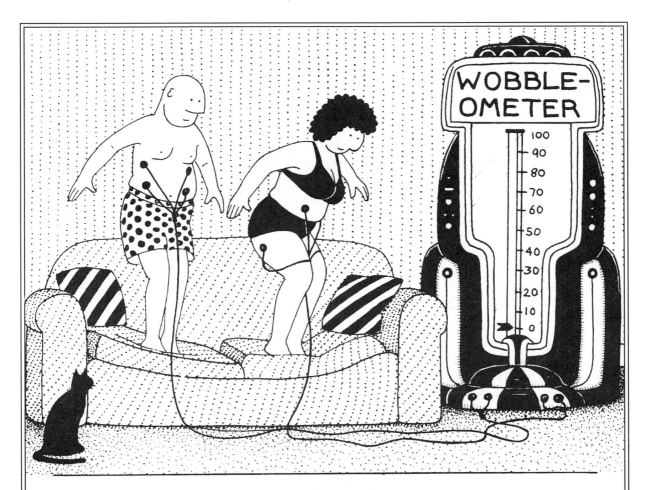

FRED AND PENELOPE FOUND THAT
BY JUMPING FROM THE SOFA THEY
COULD EASILY ACHIEVE A
MAXIMUM SCORE

FRED HAD BECOME PARTICULARLY
FOND OF D.D.I.Y. — DON'T DO
IT YOURSELF

FRED PLANNED TO SPEND THE
MORNING TESTING HIS LATEST
INVENTION : A MOTOR CAR POWERED
ENTIRELY BY NATURAL GAS

FRED WAS ALWAYS REWARDED
FOR HELPING WITH THE GROCERIES

FRED SENSED THAT PENELOPE WAS
UNHAPPY WITH HER NEW HAIRCUT

FRED AND PENELOPE COULDN'T WAIT
TO INVITE THEIR FRIENDS ROUND
TO SHOW OFF THEIR NEW LUXURY
DEEP-PILE CARPET

ALTHOUGH PENELOPE HAD NO OBJECTION
TO GETTING OLDER SHE WAS NOT
HAPPY ABOUT THE CROW'S FEET

FRED'S BARBER HAD ALWAYS
REGARDED HIM AS A TIME-WASTER

PENELOPE WAS PLEASED TO SEE
FRED AND HER MOTHER
GETTING ON FOR A CHANGE

PENELOPE SENSED THAT FRED
WAS ON TO HER

WHILE PENELOPE WARMED THE POT
FRED POPPED UPSTAIRS FOR ONE OF
HIS EXTRA-STRONG TEA BAGS

VALENTINE'S DAY COULD MEAN ONLY
ONE THING - A ROMANTIC WINDOW
TABLE FOR TWO AT FRED'S
FAVOURITE RESTAURANT

FRED WAS DELIGHTED WITH HIS NEW
SWAMP-EFFECT CARPET

'MY VERY OWN MILLENNIUM DOME',
SIGHED FRED

ON THE OCCASION OF HER BIRTHDAY
FRED INSISTED ON GIVING PENELOPE
BREAKFAST IN BED

PEOPLE COULDN'T HELP BUT BE
IMPRESSED BY FRED'S PIGEONS

FORTUNATELY FRED AND PENELOPE'S
ARGUMENT OVER WHO SHOULD HAVE
THE LAST CHOCOLATE HOBNOB
ENDED IN PEACE TALKS

IT WAS TIME FOR FRED TO HEAR
ABOUT THE BIRDS AND THE BEES

PENELOPE FOUND THAT FRED'S NEW
MALE VIRILITY PILL HAD SOME
WORRYING SIDE EFFECTS

FRED WAS DETERMINED TO MAKE
AN IMPRESSION ON THE NEW
NEXT-DOOR NEIGHBOURS

WITH THE ASSISTANCE OF A FEW
FRIENDS FRED FINALLY UNVEILED HIS
LATEST LABOUR-SAVING CREATION,
THE SIX-HEADED HAMMER

FRED AND PENELOPE DIDNT OFTEN
FIGHT BUT WHEN THEY DID IT WAS
USUALLY OVER THE LITTLE
THINGS IN LIFE

PENELOPE WAS ALREADY
BEGINNING TO REGRET HER
NEW YEARS RESOLUTION

ALTHOUGH EVERYBODY LOVED FRED
THEY EACH HAD THEIR OWN
FAVOURITE BIT

CONSTANCE GENEROUSLY OFFERED
TO HELP PENELOPE GET FRED TO
HIS DENTAL APPOINTMENT

FRED AND PENELOPE FREQUENTLY
GOT LOST BETWEEN THE
KITCHEN AND THE LOUNGE

'I THINK THEY CALL IT THE MALE
MENOPAUSE', WHISPERED PENELOPE

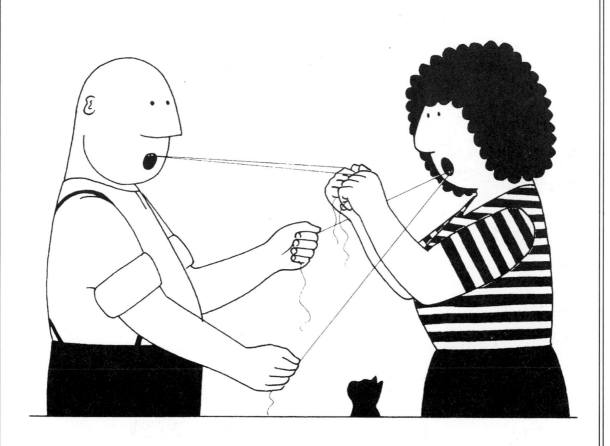

FRED AND PENELOPE LOOKED
FORWARD TO THEIR REGULAR
'FLOSSING' SESSIONS

PENELOPE BEGAN EACH DAY WITH
A FEW MINUTES PRAYER AT
HER SHRINE TO GLADYS, THE
PATRON SAINT OF SHOPPING

FRED AND PENELOPE SENSED THAT
THIS WAS NO ORDINARY MOUSE

FRED AND PIP SEEMED TO HAVE
BECOME A LOT CLOSER SINCE
PIP'S LOTTERY WIN

WHEN FRED AND PENELOPE SET OUT
FOR THEIR MEETING WITH THE LOCAL
PLANNING OFFICER IT WAS WITH
A SENSE OF FOREBODING

DOWN WITH EVERYTHING

IT WAS EARLY DAYS FOR FRED'S
POLITICAL CAREER

FRED AND PENELOPE LOVED TO TAKE
OFF INTO THE COUNTRYSIDE ON
THEIR EXERCISE BIKES

PENELOPE REALISED SHE HAD BEEN
A FOOL TO LET FRED CHOOSE THE
HOLIDAY DESTINATION

APPARENTLY MR NESBIT'S DOCTOR
HAD RECOMMENDED NO MORE THAN
ONE GLASS OF BEER PER DAY

'IT LOOKS LIKE A SIMPLE CASE OF
ONE MINCE PIE TOO MANY',
CONCLUDED THE DOCTOR

THERE WERE MOMENTS ON THE
CYCLING HOLIDAY WHEN PENELOPE
WISHED FRED COULD PEDAL JUST
THAT LITTLE BIT HARDER

FRED HAD NEVER BEEN A GREAT
ONE FOR BIRTHDAY CELEBRATIONS

IT WAS ANOTHER OF FRED'S
MECHANIC DREAMS

'IT'S THE PRIME MINISTER AGAIN',
SIGHED PENELOPE

FRED'S DINNER GUESTS MADE THE
MISTAKE OF ARRIVING FIVE
MINUTES LATE

FRED FOUND THAT BY USING AN
INFLATABLE REPLICA HE COULD
POP OUT TO THE PUB WITHOUT
PENELOPE NOTICING HE WAS GONE

IT WAS WHILST DIGGING HIS ALLOTMENT
THAT FRED ACCIDENTALLY UNEARTHED
THE ANCIENT REMAINS OF A TEMPLE
OF WORSHIP TO THE SUN GOD, RA

FRED AND PENELOPE WERE GREAT
BELIEVERS IN FORWARD PLANNING

FRED NEVER WENT ANYWHERE
WITHOUT HIS MOBILE

UNFORTUNATELY FOR FRED THERE HAD
BEEN A BIT OF A MIX-UP DOWN
AT THE STRIPPAGRAM AGENCY

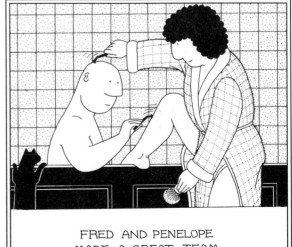

FRED AND PENELOPE
MADE A GREAT TEAM

FRED AND PENELOPE WERE
DELIGHTED TO DISCOVER THAT
THE NEW NEXT-DOOR NEIGHBOURS
WERE THEIR KIND OF PEOPLE

PENELOPE'S MODEL OF THE BANK
MANAGER WAS A REMARKABLY
GOOD LIKENESS

PENELOPE WAS FULL OF ADMIRATION
FOR FRED'S DEDICATION TO THE
NEIGHBOURHOOD WATCH SCHEME

FRED HAD OFTEN WONDERED WHAT
PENELOPE GOT UP TO IN THE CELLAR

FRED COULDN'T WAIT TO PRESENT HIS
LATEST INVENTION, 'SYNCHRONISED
PADDLING' TO THE INTERNATIONAL
OLYMPIC FEDERATION

FRED FELT HIS CHRISTMAS GUESTS
HAD OVERSTAYED THEIR WELCOME

FOR THEIR THIRD COURSE FRED
OPTED FOR THE CHEESEBOARD
WHILE PENELOPE HAD THE
SWEET TROLLEY

FRED HAD VARIOUS METHODS FOR
GETTING RID OF UNWANTED GUESTS

OVER THE YEARS FRED GOT
USED TO PENELOPE'S
VERBAL DIARRHOEA

PENELOPE AND THE GIRLS HAD
JUST ABOUT GIVEN UP ON THEIR
CELLULITE WHEN THEY DISCOVERED
THE FULL-SPIN METHOD

EVERYONE CONGRATULATED MRS NESBIT
ON MANAGING A WHOLE YEAR
WITHOUT A CIGARETTE

PENELOPE WONDERED IF THERE REALLY WOULD BE A MARKET FOR FRED'S LATEST INVENTION, THE HANDS-FREE BREAD KNIFE.

IN FRED'S CASE ONE PSYCHOTHERAPIST WAS NOT ENOUGH

FRED FOUND THE PERFECT PLACE TO BE FOR THE MILLENNIUM CELEBRATIONS

THEY DIDN'T CALL FRED 'SILENT-BUT-DEADLY-FRED' FOR NOTHING

PENELOPE SEEMED DISAPPOINTED
WITH HER NEW MOBILE PHONE

PENELOPE COULDN'T HELP FEELING
THAT FRED WAS OVER-REACTING
TO HER CREDIT CARD STATEMENT

FRED CHOSE TO IGNORE PENELOPE'S
SUGGESTION THAT HE GET
THE POOL FIRST

JUST FOR A CHANGE FRED AND
PENELOPE DECIDED TO TAKE A
DIFFERENT ROUTE HOME FROM TESCOS